D1306709

Personal Drones

by Tyler Mason

Cover: Inexpensive quadcopter drones can provide steady platforms for aerial photography.

Norwood House Press
P.O. Box 316598
Chicago, Illinois 60631

For information regarding Norwood House Press, please visit our website at:
www.norwoodhousepress.com or call 866-565-2900.

Content Consultant: John Robbins, Unmanned Aircraft Systems Program Coordinator & Associate Professor, Embry-Riddle Aeronautical University

Hardcover ISBN: 978-1-59953-937-9
Paperback ISBN: 978-1-68404-216-6

© 2019 by Norwood House Press.

Library of Congress Cataloging-in-Publication Data

Names: Mason, Tyler, author.
Title: Personal drones / Tyler Mason.
Description: Chicago, Illinois : Norwood House Press, [2018] | Series: Tech
  bytes. High-tech | Includes bibliographical references and index.
Identifiers: LCCN 2018004395 (print) | LCCN 2018011783 (ebook) | ISBN
  9781684042210 (ebook) | ISBN 9781599539379 (hardcover : alk. paper) | ISBN
  9781684042166 (pbk. : alk. paper)
Subjects: LCSH: Drone aircraft--Juvenile literature.
Classification: LCC TL685.35 (ebook) | LCC TL685.35 .M37 2018 (print) | DDC
  629.133/39--dc23
LC record available at https://lccn.loc.gov/2018004395

312N—072018
Manufactured in the United States of America in North Mankato, Minnesota.

CONTENTS

Note: Words that are **bolded** in the text are defined in the glossary.

CHAPTER 1

The History of Personal Drones

Alicia is getting ready for her hike up Mount Monadnock in southern New Hampshire. She's bringing along a map and a bottle of water. But she has another important piece of equipment. Tucked under her arm is a personal drone.

It is autumn. The trees have turned brilliant shades of red, orange, and yellow. Alicia wants to see the fall colors as the birds do—from the air. In the past, people have rented helicopters or airplanes to take **aerial** photos. But this can be expensive. A hot air balloon ride is another option. But few people have hot air balloons. Plus, they are difficult to fly.

Personal drone technology has made it easier than ever to take pictures from the sky. The average person can now see things from a bird's-eye view. Drones are amazing machines that are changing the way people see the world around them.

After an hour or so, Alicia finally reaches the top of the mountain. She finds a clear spot to launch her drone. First, she turns on the drone's camera. Then, she places the drone on a large slab of rock.

She pushes a button on her controller. The drone's propellers start whirring. Soon, the drone is hundreds of feet above her. It is recording video of the landscape. Later, Alicia will review the video on her computer at home. She'll get to see the beautiful fall foliage from the sky.

Drones give pilots—and hikers—a bird's-eye view.

What Are Personal Drones?

Drones are also known as unmanned aerial systems. These devices fly without a pilot on board. Usually, people on the ground remotely control drones. Some drones are large and powerful. The military uses drones to monitor enemies during war. A few can even launch weapons. But most drones are much smaller and less powerful than military drones. They are known as personal drones.

Most personal drones are quadcopter drones. Quadcopters do not fly the way an airplane flies. They fly more similarly to a helicopter. A quadcopter drone has four propellers. Two propellers have motors that spin clockwise. The other two have motors that spin counterclockwise. The motors that spin in the same direction are diagonally across from each other. Controllers speed up or slow down the motors to move the drone.

Quadcopters have four different ranges of motion. They can move up and down. They can tilt left and right. They can also tilt forward and backward. Finally, they can rotate clockwise and counterclockwise.

Tilting the drone left and right is called roll. Tilting it forward and backward is called pitch. Rotating it clockwise or counterclockwise is called yaw. Spinning propellers give the drone **lift**. That lift allows the drone to get off the ground and go up and down. A pilot on the ground controls all these different motions.

An important technology used by quadcopter drones is the global positioning system, or GPS. GPS involves a group of satellites that orbit Earth. They send signals to the ground. A GPS receiver listens for these signals. It knows where each satellite is, and it knows exactly when it received each signal. The receiver uses this information to determine its precise location. A drone with GPS can maintain its position, even in strong winds. The GPS also helps the drone land in the same location from which it took off.

Not all personal drones are quadcopters. Fixed-wing drones are another type of personal drone. These drones look more similar to an airplane than a quadcopter.

Quadcopters have four propellers. They often have a video camera, too.

They can fly for longer amounts of time than quadcopters, too.

The First Drones

The military developed and used the first drones. The earliest drones date back to World War I (1914–1918). Charles Kettering developed the Kettering

The Kettering Bug, developed during World War I, is considered the first drone.

Bug in 1918. The US Army tested the Kettering Bug. It could carry bombs to distant targets without a pilot. But it was never actually used in battle.

Today, the military uses drones for surveillance and for attacking enemy forces. They have fierce names such as Predator, Reaper, and Global Hawk.

These drones can travel hundreds or even thousands of miles at a time. They cost millions of dollars to build. Military drones and personal quadcopter drones have some things in common. Both types of drones often have cameras on board. And they are both piloted by humans on the ground.

The first popular quadcopter drone came onto the scene in the 2000s. Parrot introduced its AR.Drone at the Consumer Electronics Show in 2010. It received plenty of interest as one of the first consumer quadcopters.

Pilots controlled the AR.Drone with their smartphones. But it had limited functions. Some pilots found it hard to fly. The drone was not intended to be used professionally. Parrot said it designed the drone as a toy. Since then, the company has created other drones. But it is facing more competition from other drone manufacturers.

Many new manufacturers have entered the drone market. Chinese company DJI introduced its first Phantom drone in January 2013. Rival company Yuneec unveiled the Typhoon Q500 in 2014. It was the company's first personal drone

DID YOU KNOW?

DJI stands for Dajiang Innovation Technology Co. The company's headquarters are in Shenzhen, China.

Drone Market Domination

Drone manufacturers are all fighting for a slice of the drone industry. But one company has dominated the competition. DJI has produced more personal drones than any other company. In 2017, approximately 70 percent of personal drones were DJI products. They included the Phantom, Mavic, Osmo, Spark, and Inspire. DJI is now the most recognizable brand in personal drones. The company has offices on three continents throughout the world.

on the market. 3DR's Solo drone was released in 2015. GoPro, a company known for making tiny cameras, released its own drone in late 2016.

The price of these drones varies greatly. Small toy drones without cameras cost approximately $40. Common models such as the DJI Phantom or Mavic sell for approximately $1,000. Drones used for movies and television can cost tens of thousands of dollars, with expensive cameras sold separately.

There are many great drones on the market today. But some drone pilots choose to build their own quadcopters. They purchase the motors, batteries, frames, flight controllers, cameras, and other parts. They follow plans they download from the Internet. Summer camps and high school classes teach pilots how to build and fly drones, too.

Uses for Personal Drones

Personal drones are used for many things today. Lots of drone pilots enjoy taking pictures and videos for fun. Other pilots fly drones for a career. Some people use personal drones for search and rescue missions. Drones fly over disaster areas searching for survivors. Farmers use drones to monitor their crops. They can check how well their crops are growing. Some drone pilots race custom-built quadcopters that fly at high speeds. They feel like they are in the air themselves as the quadcopters race across the sky.

In the time since the first quadcopter drones became available, companies have made many technological innovations. Today, drones can shoot high-resolution video. Every frame is crystal clear. Many personal drones have stabilized cameras. The cameras are secured by a **gimbal**. The gimbal smooths out the video, even

? DID YOU KNOW?

GoPro's first drone, the Karma, was taken off the market for a few months. Many of the drones fell out of the sky. GoPro said it was an issue with the drone's battery.

FPV Drones

Most personal drones have a top speed of around 45 miles per hour (72 kmh). A special type of quadcopter flies even faster. Racing drones can fly at up to 120 miles per hour (193 kmh). They are often referred to as **first-person view** (FPV) drones. Pilots who fly these racing drones wear goggles. The goggles display the view of the camera on the front of the drone. Pilots often build their own FPV drones. They create custom parts to build their unique quadcopters.

when the drone is moving. Some drones have **sensors** to detect and avoid objects. This helps the drones avoid crashing into people, buildings, or other aircraft.

Today's drones are smaller, too. One good example is the DJI Mavic. It takes high-quality video. But it is very small. The drone can fit inside a backpack, a purse, or even a pocket. Pilots can take it with them on vacation or on a hike.

A 2016 rule created by the **Federal Aviation Administration** (FAA) made it easier for personal drone pilots to fly commercially in the United States. Pilots take a test to receive their remote pilot certificate. Those who pass can turn their hobby into a business.

Sales of personal drones show how much the industry is growing. Approximately 2.8 million personal

Personal drones are fun for adults and kids alike.

drones were sold in 2016. The number is expected to reach 6.6 million in 2020.

Drones are a rapidly advancing technology. More and more drones will enter the airspace. Rules about flying drones will evolve. The technology will improve, too. One thing is certain: drones are here to stay.

CHAPTER 2

Challenges in the Air

Drones have come a long way since the first quadcopters. Cameras are higher quality. Flight times are longer. And drone software improvements have made them much easier to fly. Today, anyone can buy a drone online or at an electronics store. No training is required to fly a drone. That can be a good and bad thing for the future of drones.

More drones are taking to the skies. Governments are trying to decide how to regulate drones. It is a complicated process. Drone pilots face plenty of hurdles today. And rules and regulations are always changing.

Passing the Test

Drone pilots can make money flying their drones. Commercial drone pilots fly for lots of different jobs. Some fly for television shows or movies. Some take pictures of houses for real estate agents. Others use drones for inspections.

Real estate agents use drones to take pictures of homes for sale.

All pilots flying drones commercially must be licensed. It does not matter what type of job they are doing. They have to pass a test before they can fly commercially. The FAA requires pilots to take the test. It is commonly referred to as Part 107.

The FAA introduced the Part 107 test in August 2016. The test is made up of 60 multiple-choice questions. Pilots who take the test must know a variety of subjects. They have to know how to read aviation maps and find accurate weather forecasts. They must know emergency procedures and be aware of drone rules. By September 2017, more than 60,000 pilots had passed the Part 107 test.

The Part 107 test is easier than the previous certification process. It was called the 333 exemption. Applicants needed to have a regular pilot's license before becoming licensed to fly commercial drones.

Following the Rules

Many rules determine where drones can and cannot fly in the United States. The FAA regulates these rules. Different rules apply to personal drone pilots and commercial drone pilots. Pilots who do not follow these rules may have to pay a fine. Other offenders may get jail time.

Drone pilots must keep their drones below 400 feet (122 m). Drones are not allowed to fly directly over people. There are rules for flying close to airports, too. Personal drone pilots must notify an airport before flying within 5 miles (8 km)

? DID YOU KNOW?

Drone pilots who obtain their remote pilot certificate must retake the test every two years. Pilots must be at least 16 years old to take the test.

Security Sensitive Airspace

Drones cannot fly over sensitive areas of the United States. Security sensitive areas include the White House and military bases across the country. It is illegal to fly a drone over these areas for any purpose, 24 hours a day, seven days a week. The restriction extends from the ground to 400 feet (122 m) above ground level. It is very difficult to obtain an exception to these rules. Without special permission, pilots who fly in security sensitive airspace may be fined up to $250,000 and may serve jail time.

of it. Commercial operators must get permission to fly in certain areas. It can take 90 days or more before pilots get approval. That can be a problem for commercial pilots who need to fly in **restricted airspace** on short notice.

The FAA has worked to make this process easier for commercial pilots. It announced the Low Altitude Authorization and Notification Capability (LAANC) in 2017. Certified pilots can use LAANC to instantly get permission to fly in certain restricted airspace.

Pilots must always be able to see their drone while they are flying. This is called visual line of sight (VLOS). Some personal drones can fly farther than the eye can see, though. The DJI Mavic can travel up to 8 miles (13 km) away from the pilot. As these drones become more

Drones at Sporting Events

The FAA creates **temporary flight restrictions** over stadiums during games. They take effect one hour before the game and end one hour after the game is done. Some pilots have flown drones over stadiums during games even though it is illegal. They have often paid the price for it. A man was arrested in November 2017 when he flew his drone over a football game in California. He used his drone to drop pamphlets from the sky. Other drone pilots have flown over games to take pictures or video. They have also been fined.

popular, the FAA may need to change its rules. The requirement of flying within the pilot's sight could change. Drones may be able to fly beyond VLOS. That would open up more possibilities for drone companies.

Other rules limit where drone pilots can fly. Drones cannot operate in national parks in the United States without a permit. That way, everyone can enjoy the parks without the whirr of a drone's propellers. The city of Washington, DC, has a large no-fly zone surrounding it. This is to protect federal buildings and political leaders. The FAA has also banned drones from flying over the Statue of Liberty and other landmarks. No-fly zones are in effect during professional and college athletic events. Drones cannot fly within 3 miles (5 km) of a stadium during

? DID YOU KNOW?

Drones have been banned from national parks in the United States since 2014. However, pilots can legally fly over national parks as long as the drone takes off and lands outside the park's boundaries.

a professional football or baseball game. They cannot fly over a college football game or a NASCAR race.

Some cities have rules for where drones can and cannot fly. In 2015, Chicago, Illinois, passed an ordinance that bans

Some people worry that drones may invade their privacy.

drones from flying over public property. Other cities, such as Minneapolis, Minnesota, do not allow drones to take off or land from city parks.

What the Public Thinks

From monitoring crops to fun videos, there are lots of examples of drones being used for good. Still, many people think drones are bad or scary. Some do not support the use of drones for any reason.

Privacy is a primary concern. Some people believe pilots will use drones to spy on them. Drones could hover near homes or yards. Their high-resolution cameras could zoom in on homeowners and their families. Cities throughout the

United States and in other countries work to prevent drones from spying.

Sometimes, people take extreme measures against drones. Many drones have been destroyed by neighbors. Those who destroy them often feel their privacy is being invaded. However, destroying a drone is a federal crime. Drones are considered aircraft.

Limitations of Drone Technology

Drone technology has improved greatly since 2010. However, there are still technological limits of drone flights. One of the biggest obstacles is the battery life. Most personal drones can fly for just 15 to 30 minutes on a single battery charge. Flight times can become even shorter in extreme heat or cold.

Drone companies work to improve battery life. This helps drones fly for longer periods at a time. A company called Skyfront introduced the Tailwind drone in September 2017. It is a **hybrid** drone that uses gasoline and electric power. The Tailwind flew for more than four hours. Skyfront is working to improve battery life to more than five hours.

Solar-powered drones are also being developed. Facebook has created a large solar-powered drone called Aquila. It is designed to provide Internet service to remote locations. But the Aquila is not a personal drone. Other large-scale drones have used solar power to fly for long periods. But solar-powered personal drones are still not available to purchase.

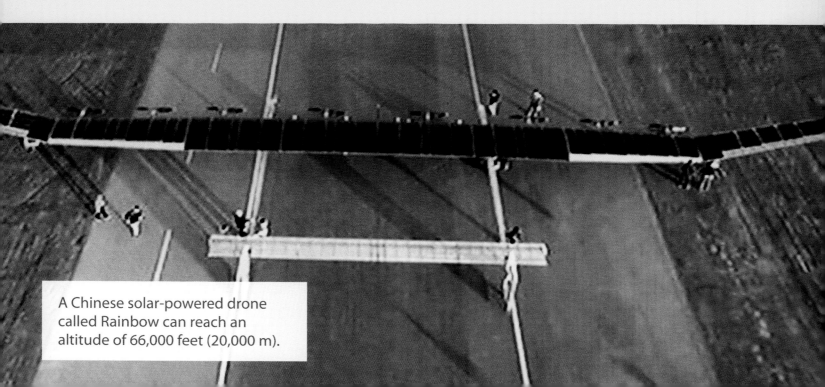

A Chinese solar-powered drone called Rainbow can reach an altitude of 66,000 feet (20,000 m).

CHAPTER 3

More Than Toys

Drones can be lots of fun. But they are more than just toys. Many people today use drones as tools. Drones take pictures to help farmers with crops. They perform industrial inspections. Engineers think up new uses for drones every day.

Cameras That Fly

The most popular use of personal drones is photography and videography. Many personal drone pilots use their drones

Photographers use drones to capture bird's-eye views of weddings.

Drones and the News

CNN is a pioneer for drones in journalism. It was one of the first news outlets to use drones. CNN created CNN Aerial Imagery and Reporting (CNN AIR) in August 2016. CNN AIR helps the network include drones in its reporting. It has worked closely with the FAA to help set up drone guidelines for newsrooms. The network was the first organization to get permission from the FAA to fly over people. The FAA requires CNN to fly a drone called Snap. The Snap drone is lightweight. It has protected propellers for safety. CNN uses drones to show footage of natural disasters, war zones, and remote locations.

only for taking pictures or videos. They can see their city or home from a new perspective. They can share these images with friends and family.

Professional drone pilots make money by taking aerial photographs and videos. Many commercial drone pilots take real estate photography. These aerial images show a house or property from above. People attending weddings may now notice something flying in the sky. Drones are popular tools for photographers to capture wedding images. But the noise of a drone can be distracting during a wedding ceremony. They are usually used after the ceremony. The drone snaps pictures of the wedding party and guests.

Several film festivals exclusively feature drone videos. They include the New York City Drone Film Festival

Drones from the technology company Intel created a light show outside a Las Vegas, Nevada, hotel in 2018.

and the Flying Robot International Film Festival. These festivals award prizes to a variety of categories. The common theme is that all of the films are shot with a drone.

Television and movie companies now use drones to capture certain camera angles. These types of shots might have previously required helicopters. Drones are much cheaper. They are also usually safer than a helicopter. The drones used in Hollywood are sometimes personal drones. But many are much bigger and more expensive than the drones available to average consumers.

Drones have become valuable tools for modern journalists. Newspapers and television stations use drones to provide a different view of current events. Journalists have used drones to capture

Artful Drones

Drones often take artistic pictures and videos from the sky. But drones themselves have become the subject of the art. Approximately 300 drones flew during the Super Bowl LI half-time show in 2017. Each was lit in red, white, or blue. They formed an American flag during Lady Gaga's performance. The drones flew in a pattern that was programmed by computers. Walt Disney World has created similar drone light shows. One of the park's most popular is its holiday show.

images of protests. They have flown drones over the devastation caused by natural disasters. Many newsrooms now have a certified remote pilot on staff.

Drones can stream their video live to the Internet. Some drones stream footage directly to Facebook or YouTube. These videos are great resources for journalists covering a live event. However, most drones do not record audio. Drone propellers make too much noise; however, some drones allow pilots to record audio through the drone's controller. Pilots can describe what they are viewing on the live stream.

Drones for Good

Personal drones can save lives. Search and rescue missions now often include a drone. The drone flies high and over long distances. This is helpful for rescuing a lost family member or pet. The drone may also use a special camera to help see people at night.

There are many success stories of drones being used to save lives. Police found an elderly man in Minnesota with the help of a drone. The police department used a drone with a **thermal imaging** camera. The camera used heat instead of light to create an image. The man's body heat lit up the camera. The police were able to find him. A search and rescue team in Iowa used a drone to find a group of six people. Another rescue team found two missing hikers and their dog with a drone. These are just a few examples of search and rescue missions that used drones.

A first responder pilots a drone in the search for survivors after an earthquake in Ecuador in 2016.

Scientists use drones to monitor animal habitats. Conservation Drones is a group that does just that. They use drones to keep an eye on tigers in India. The tigers are an endangered species. But people illegally hunt them for sport and money. The drones help Conservation Drones catch these hunters. Other scientists use

Scientists in South Africa's Hluhluwe-Imfolozi Game Reserve use drones to study threatened wildlife.

drones to study orangutans in Sumatra, Indonesia. The drones allow the researchers to see whether the orangutans' habitats are shrinking.

Drones have also been used to study whales. Scientists fly a drone close to a whale's blowhole. It hovers above the blowhole, waiting for the whale to breathe out. When it does, the drone collects the snotty spray. The drone has the nickname Snot Bot. Scientists can study the spray to learn about the whale's health.

Fire departments use drones to help with many different things. Firefighters fly drones around burning homes. Thermal cameras on the drones can show where fire is spreading. Firefighters use the image to know where to enter burning buildings.

Police officers use drones as well. Drones help police find suspects on the run. Police departments also use drones to monitor traffic. Drones help detectives investigate crime scenes. Police departments in nearly every state in the United States use drones.

Industrial Uses for Personal Drones

Personal drones can be effective for a variety of industrial and agricultural uses. Farmers fly drones from their front steps to survey their crops. They use the drones' cameras to see remote areas of the field. They analyze the image to know what crops need to be watered. This can save farmers lots of time. Without the drone, a farmer would have to walk along the field to monitor the crops. In the past, farmers would hire airplanes to fly over their fields. But this was expensive. Using a drone is cheaper than renting a plane.

Some agricultural drones do more than just photograph crops. Some drones can spread fertilizer on fields. Pilots program the drones with special software. The software tells the drones to fly in specific patterns while spraying fertilizer.

Another use for personal drones is mapping. Software applications make it very easy for a pilot to map a wide

A drone sprays fertilizer on a rice field.

area of land. One example of a software application with this capability is DroneDeploy. It allows the pilot to select the route on the screen of the controller. The end result is a 3-D map of the area. Many personal drones are capable of mapping with this technology.

Some pilots use drones to perform inspections. Drones can inspect long oil pipelines. Engineers no longer have to manually inspect the pipelines. Roof inspections are safer with a drone. Using a drone eliminates the need for a contractor to climb up onto a roof. Civil engineers use drones to inspect bridges.

Advertising with drones has become common. Some companies have created drones that can display a message or slogan. These drones either carry a

DID YOU KNOW?

Many drone pilots upload drone videos to the web. Some websites exclusively feature aerial footage and images from drones.

banner or use a light-up display. Drone advertising gives companies a unique way to promote their businesses.

Flying Fast with Mini Quadcopters

Another popular use of drones is drone racing. Pilots custom build mini quadcopters. These drones are smaller

A drone flies over the course of a Ukrainian drone race in 2017.

than camera drones. They fly much faster. The fastest one of these drones has flown is 163 miles per hour (262 kmh).

Pilots who fly mini quads do two different types of flying. Some compete in races. They fly their drones around a marked course. Other pilots fly freestyle. They navigate their drones through tricks, spins, and flips in the air. Freestyle pilots often fly their drones in abandoned buildings or through forests.

Many different racing leagues have been created as the sport became popular. The Drone Racing League showcases the sport on ESPN. Other leagues include DR1, the International Drone Racing Association, and MultiGP. Most drone racing pilots fly in races organized in their area. Top pilots compete in national and international races. Some of the best drone racing pilots make money by winning races.

Some pilots fly drones that are even smaller than mini quads. These small quadcopters can still fly fast. A tiny camera on front gives the pilot the drone's view. They are much safer than larger quadcopters to fly in small spaces and indoors. They are made of plastic. Their propellers have guards to protect them.

DID YOU KNOW?

The DJI Spark drone can be controlled with hand motions. The drone has sensors that pick up the pilot's hand gestures showing where the drone should fly.

CHAPTER 4

Future Drone Tech

Drone technology has improved tremendously in a relatively short period. Drones are more common than ever. It can be exciting to think about the future of drones. How far can this technology advance? What new ways will people find to use drones?

As they evolve, drones will have to overcome several issues. Drone rules and laws will continue to change. Public perception of drones will need to improve. And with more pilots taking to the sky, other issues could arise.

Improving Technology

Most drones today shoot 4K video. This type of video has very high resolution. Images are very sharp and crystal clear. That is a big improvement over the cameras on early personal quadcopters. These early drones often did not even have stabilized cameras. Video was grainy and shaky.

A drone equipped with a 4K camera

But drone video quality will improve past 4K. Some drones can take better than 4K video. Commercial drones used for movies and TV shows sometimes use cameras that are four times as powerful as 4K. But the average pilot does not fly

Colleges now offer degrees in drone technology.

these kinds of drones. Some pilots use 360-degree cameras on drones. This gives viewers the ability to see things in every direction. A company called Aerial Pro 360 claims it created the first drone that shoots 360-degree video in 4K resolution.

Drones in Education

High school and college students can now study drones in school. High school classes teach kids how to build a drone from scratch. Summer camps also educate kids on how to fly drones. Some colleges offer degrees in drones. The Embry-Riddle Aeronautical University in Daytona Beach, Florida, has the largest unmanned aerial systems program. More than 1,000 students are enrolled in the drone program. Students at Kansas State Polytechnic can get a degree in unmanned aircraft systems. The University of North Dakota's aviation department lets students major in unmanned aircraft systems operations. More schools are including similar drone programs.

The ability to take 360-degree video gives pilots many more options for filming.

Drones will continue to be built with more advanced features. Obstacle avoidance technology continues to improve on personal drones. DJI is developing advanced obstacle avoidance technology. It uses cameras, sensors, and computer **algorithms**. These things work together to tell the drone if there is an obstacle in its path. Flight times on personal drones are also improving. Most personal drone pilots measure flight times in minutes, not hours. But drone companies are developing better motors and batteries.

Drone taxi Volocopter 2X on display in Dubai, United Arab Emirates, in 2017

Drone Taxis and Other Transportation

Imagine waiting for a taxi that does not drive up the street but instead drops from the sky. Some experts believe drones will become a common mode of transportation. Riders would get into a giant drone instead of a car. These drones would be much bigger than the average personal drone. But they could become a personal drone to those who could afford to own one.

DID YOU KNOW?

Canada has stricter drone laws than the United States. Canadian pilots can only fly up to 300 feet (90 m) above the ground. Drones must also stay 250 feet (76 m) from people, buildings, or vehicles.

Drone taxis have been tested around the world. A German company called Volocopter has designed a drone taxi. It has 18 rotors and a parachute for emergencies. The company tested the drone in Dubai, in the United Arab Emirates, in September 2017. The Volocopter flew for five minutes during the test. It soared approximately 650 feet (200 m) above the ground. The drone's passenger was Sheikh Hamdan bin Mohammed, the Crown Prince of Dubai. Dubai hopes to have 25 percent of its taxi riders flying in these drones by 2030.

Other companies have developed similar transportation drones. Chinese company Ehang introduced the Ehang 184. It can fly for 25 minutes. The Ehang 184 has a top speed of 62 miles per hour (100 kmh).

Evolving Regulations

Drone laws are always changing. It has become easier to fly a drone commercially. What may the future hold for federal and state drone rules?

DID YOU KNOW?

Technology research company Gartner predicts the drone industry will be worth $11 billion by 2020. That includes personal and commercial drones.

Delivery by Drone

The future of package delivery may include drones. Amazon and UPS have drone technologies in development. Both have tested delivery services using drones. Amazon's drone service is called Amazon Air. The company says it can deliver packages of 5 pounds (2 kg) or less in under 30 minutes. It has tested the technology in several countries. UPS's drone delivery system works alongside trucks. The drone launches from the top of a UPS truck to deliver a package. The flight time of the UPS drone is 30 minutes. Federal laws may have to change before drone deliveries become a reality. A drone currently cannot fly out of a pilot's line of sight. That would be necessary for long-range deliveries.

In the future, all drones may be allowed to fly over people. It is currently very hard to get permission to fly over people legally. Only a few companies have received it. Usually, being granted permission comes with strict guidelines. But flying drones over people could be necessary. Many companies have designed parachute systems for drones. These parachutes can help a drone fall slowly to the ground. This could prevent major injuries to people on the ground.

Today, drone pilots must have permission to fly their drone out of their sight. The technology to fly drones out of sight exists. But the regulations need to catch up with the technology.

Amazon tests its drone package delivery service in Germany.

Drones flying near airplanes will remain a concern. Several drones have come close to hitting airplanes. This could continue to be a problem as more drone pilots take to the sky. It is hard to know who is flying these drones in dangerous

Today, students can learn all about building and piloting drones.

areas. Manufacturer DJI created one way to identify these drones. The system is called DJI AeroScope. It uses the drone's signal to broadcast important information. Police departments and others can access this information. They use it to identify pilots and their locations.

Who Patrols the Skies?

The FAA regulates all drone flights in the United States. Cities and states want to have a say in making rules for drones, too. But most cities have been unsuccessful in doing so.

The town of Newton, Massachusetts, previously banned drones from flying. The rule prevented drones from flying over property without permission. It also required pilots to register their drones. Those rules were eventually changed.

Newton was sued by a drone pilot who lives in the town. He argued that drone pilots must follow the FAA's drone laws and not the town's local rules. A judge agreed. He ruled the FAA governs the airspace drones fly in. The lawsuit may prevent other towns from making similar rules. But some cities need to consider future rules specific to drones.

Rules for drones continue to evolve. Drone technology changes rapidly. The idea of more people flying drones could be scary. But it can also be exciting. It means more possibilities to create great videos. Drone pilots know one thing: the sky is the limit for the future of drones.

GLOSSARY

aerial (AIR-ee-ul): In the air or sky.

algorithms (AL-go-rith-umz): Sets of rules computers use to solve a problem.

Federal Aviation Administration (FED-ur-ul ay-vee-AY-shun ad-min-uh-STRAY-shun): The governmental body that has authority over all aviation in the United States.

first-person view (FURST PUR-sin VEW): Using goggles to see a drone camera's perspective.

gimbal (GIM-bull): A mechanism made up of rings that pivot on an axis to help keep a camera stable on a drone.

hybrid (HI-brid): A type of vehicle that uses two or more forms of energy to run.

lift (LIFT): An upward force that helps enable drones and other aircraft to fly.

restricted airspace (ree-STRIK-tud AYR-spase): Areas of airspace that require permission to fly an airplane.

sensors (SEN-surz): Devices that detect heat, light, sound, pressure, or other changes in their environments.

temporary flight restrictions (temp-ur-RAYR-ee FLYT ree-STRIK-shuns): Actions that restrict certain aircraft from flying in a particular airspace for a short period of time for a special occasion or sporting event.

thermal imaging (THUR-mul IM-ij-ing): A method of using heat from an object to create an image.

FOR MORE INFORMATION

Books

Katie Marsico. *Drones*. New York: Children's Press, 2016. This book explains how drones work and how to fly one.

Laurie Newman. *Drones*. Ann Arbor, MI: Cherry Lake Publishing, 2018. Check out a timeline of drone history and discover more about these amazing devices.

Steven Otfinoski. *Drones: Science, Technology, and Engineering*. New York: Scholastic, 2017. This book explores the history of drones and looks at the many uses of these flying machines.

Websites

The Different Kinds of Drones (http://www.pbs.org/independentlens/blog/a-drone-by-any-other-name-what-are-the-different-kinds-of-drones/) Learn more about all sorts of drones, from large military drones to mini quadcopters.

Drones to the Rescue (https://www.kidsdiscover.com/teacherresources/drones-uavs-rescue/) Discover more about all the good things drones do for people.

Kids, Drones, and Science (https://blog.nature.org/science/2017/08/07/grenada-reef-week-drones-schill-grenville-resilience/) Learn how kids participated in a project to use drones to help the environment on the coast of Grenada.

ABOUT THE AUTHOR

Tyler Mason is a certified remote pilot and has been flying drones since August 2015. He studied journalism at the University of Wisconsin–Madison. Mason is the director of a drone media sharing website. He currently lives in Hudson, Wisconsin, with his wife.